NEW ORLEANS VOODOO

ELDORADO INK

The Supernatural

Witches and Wicca

Haunted Places and Ghostly Encounters

New Orleans Voodoo

Shamans, Witch Doctors, Wizards, Sorcerers, and Alchemists

The Undead: Vampires, Zombies, and other Strange Monsters

Legendary Creatures

Unexplained Monsters and Cryptids

Angels, Demons, and Religious Rituals

THE SUPERNATURAL

NEW ORLEANS VOODOO

BY CAROL ELLIS

ELDORADO INK

Eldorado Ink
PO Box 100097
Pittsburgh, PA 15233
www.eldoradoink.com

Produced by OTTN Publishing, Stockton, New Jersey

CPSIA compliance information: Batch#S2015.
For further information, contact Eldorado Ink at info@eldoradoink.com.

First printing

1 3 5 7 9 8 6 4 2

Library of Congress Cataloging-in-Publication Data

  Applied for
    ISBN 978-1-61900-068-1 (hc)
    ISBN 978-1-61900-076-6 (trade) •
    ISBN 978-1-61900-084-1 (ebook)

*For information about custom editions, special sales, or premiums,
please contact our special sales department at info@eldoradoink.com.*

TABLE OF CONTENTS

CURSE OF THE SUPERDOME

It was December 30, 2000. Inside the New Orleans Superdome, all eyes were on the 50-yard line. The woman standing there had a large spotted snake draped around her neck. She was a Voodoo priestess, and she was there to help the New Orleans Saints win the football game they were about to play against the defending Super Bowl champions, the Saint Louis Rams.

The Saints had not won a playoff game since 1971, when the Superdome was built. It had been a long 29 years, and there were many possible reasons for the team's shortcomings: abominable management, bad coaching, poor play, inevitable injuries. But one other possibility kept coming up: maybe the stadium was cursed.

DISRESPECTED SPIRITS

The problem with the Superdome was the location. When backhoes ripped into the ground at the start of its construction, they tore up

---

In 2000, the New Orleans Saints football team called on Voodoo priestess Ava Kay Jones (pictured in inset) to help them break a supposed curse on their home field, the Louisiana Superdome.

what had once been sacred, consecrated ground. It was the site of the old Girod Street Cemetery, a graveyard where victims of yellow fever and cholera epidemics had been buried for more than 120 years.

It wasn't that the construction crew just dug into an existing cemetery in an unorganized, unplanned way. The Girod Street Cemetery had fallen into disrepair and neglect over the years. It had been deconsecrated and closed. Care had been taken to move human remains to other sites to make way for new construction, including the Superdome. But when the digging began, human bones, as well as wooden and tin caskets, were found. It was obvious that not all the remains had been found or relocated.

LI GRAND ZOMBI

For people from New Orleans, it wasn't surprising to see Ava Kay Jones dancing with a snake at the Superdome. In many African religions, as well as in voodoo as it's practiced in New Orleans today, the snake represents a major spirit, called Li Grand Zombi. The name of this spirit is derived from Nzambi, the creator god of the Bantu and Kongo religions.

In the 19th century, American Christians often viewed voodoo with fear or outrage. Most of them associated snake dancing with devil worship, and were unaware of its connection to a spirit that was sacred to African slaves.

Today, snakes are used in Voodoo celebrations for the public and in entertainment for tourists. But they also play a part in private, religious ceremonies. Not everyone uses live snakes, of course. In fact, people are discouraged from doing it, because of the responsibility of caring for a snake, as well as the potential danger. Practitioners of Voodoo believe that like other spirits, the spirit of Li Grand Zombi can be honored with pictures or statues, candles and food.

Tombs at the Girod Street Cemetery, which was opened in New Orleans around 1822. By the mid-20th century the cemetery was not being used, and in 1957 it was closed and de-consecrated. The remains of those buried at the Girod Street Cemetery were supposed to have been moved to other places. However, some people feared that some spirits whose bodies had not been moved continued to haunt the area.

As the Saints struggled over the years, superstitious New Orleans fans began to wonder: were the spirits of the unclaimed dead still haunting the area around the Superdome? Had those spirits, unhappy about the disturbance to their final resting place, put a curse on the stadium?

These questions were almost always asked with a laugh, and were often answered with a shrug and a chuckle. Only part of the parking lot, most people said, was built on the old cemetery site. How could spirits, if there really were any, be bothered about that? On the surface, no one seemed to take the idea seriously. The Voodoo priestess and her snake were just for show—a way to hype the game so the team and local businesses could make money.

Since the curse at the Louisiana Superdome was supposedly lifted in 2000, the New Orleans Saints have been one of the NFL's more successful teams, reaching the playoffs many times and winning an NFL championship in 2010.

But the laughs and the chuckles sometimes had a nervous edge. This was New Orleans, after all. It was the home not just of a modern football team, but also of Voodoo, a practice that has its roots in old-world religions of West Africa. To those who believe in Voodoo, the spirits of the dead are always nearby and deserve respect and attention.

VOODOO IS EVERYWHERE

Say the word *Voodoo*, and many people think of dolls with pins stuck in them, curses that can harm or kill, mindless zombies, and magic charms that can bring good luck, ward off evil, or help a person gain revenge against an enemy.

If you visit New Orleans, the influence of Voodoo is hard to miss. It's everywhere you look. Shops sell candles, special ointments and

Superstitions about sports have a long history. One of the most famous was the "Curse of the Bambino." After the Boston Red Sox sold a young player named Babe Ruth to the New York Yankees in 1920, the team didn't win a World Series for the next 83 years. Athletes often have their own personal superstitions—some eat the same meal before a game, some wear the same socks, or listen to the same music. Some believe that changing even the tiniest thing might jinx a play, or the outcome of an entire game.

oils, supposedly magic amulets called gris-gris bags meant to protect their owners, and Voodoo dolls. You can visit a Voodoo museum, take tours of Voodoo-related sites, and eat mojo chicken at a Voodoo-themed restaurant. As a result, some people dismiss Voodoo as a gimmick to get tourists to part with their money. It's really just a business, they say.

Check the New Orleans yellow pages, and you'll find listings for dozens of voodoo priestesses and practitioners who offer spiritual advice. One of them is Ava Kay Jones, the woman standing on the 50-yard-line of the Superdome in December 2000. Jones seemed an unlikely person to practice a religion based on superstition and ancient beliefs. She is well educated, having been a practicing attorney before becoming a voodoo priestess. She was raised in the Roman Catholic faith, and still considers herself a good Catholic.

Perhaps the ritual that Jones performed at the stadium worked. After all, New Orleans ended up winning the game, 31 to 28. Since that day, the Saints franchise has won six more playoff games, including Super Bowl XLIV in February 2010. So now New Orleans fans can joke about how the Superdome curse has been lifted. But Jones, like many other residents of New Orleans, takes voodoo seriously. Despite the tourist aspects, Voodoo as a seriously practiced religion is alive and well in this old city.

VOODOO IN THE NEW WORLD

During the late 17th century, explorers claimed a vast North American territory, known as Louisiana, for the king of France. This region stretched from the French settlements of Montreal and Quebec in Canada through the Mississippi River valley south to the Gulf of Mexico. The first French colonists in this territory, which became known as Louisiana, found that farmland near the Mississippi River was good for growing crops like cotton, rice, and sugar cane—all products that were in demand in Europe.

But cultivating and harvesting these crops required more workers than the small French colonies could provide by themselves. So like other Europeans who settled in the New World, the French decided to use the forced labor of slaves. At first, the French enslaved Native American tribes that they encountered and could subdue. But by 1717, the colonists had begun importing African-American slaves from west and central Africa.

African slaves were desirable because their home regions were similar in climate to Louisiana, and some of the slaves had cultivated

---

An African-American family stands outside the slave quarters on a Louisiana plantation. Africans slaves brought their religious beliefs with them to the New World, including some superstitious practices that would become known as Voodoo.

rice and similar crops before being captured. The slaves brought their culture with them to the New World, such as their music with its drumming and dancing, and their religious beliefs.

TRADITIONAL RELIGIONS OF WEST AFRICA

The West African people forced into slavery hadn't grown up with a single, unified religion. After all, West Africa had never been a single, unified country. It covered a huge amount of land and was home to many different tribes and ethnic groups. Each had its own system of government, language, culture, and customs. Each tribe also had its own religious beliefs.

But even though the religions of West Africa were very different, they shared a few of the same beliefs. West Africans believed in a

Africans participate in a religious ceremony intended to honor the spirits of their ancestors, called Enungun, in Benin, West Africa. The Yoruba people, as well as others indigenous to West Africa, believe that both natural spirits and deceased ancestors have power and influence over the living.

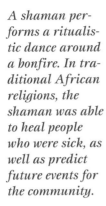

A shaman performs a ritualistic dance around a bonfire. In traditional African religions, the shaman was able to heal people who were sick, as well as predict future events for the community.

supreme god that had created the Earth and humankind. This god was distant and remote, and didn't get involved with earthly business. Spirits were in charge of that.

Spirits could be found everywhere—in plants and animals, in stones and trees, or in rivers, oceans, and lakes. Some spirits interacted between humans and the supreme god, or between humans and other spirits. Others were responsible for human affairs such as health, work, family, love, happiness, or a successful harvest.

The spirits of ancestors were also important in African religions. Africans believed that a person's spirit never dies, but remains in the community. The living looked to these ancestral spirits for guidance in their daily lives. They honored them with songs of praise in annual ceremonies, and left offerings of food and drink at their burial sites. As long as the ancestral spirits were properly honored, they would give people protection and advice. However, if they weren't properly honored, the spirits wouldn't help. They might even harm the living person who had treated them with disrespect.

An African who was experiencing illness or bad fortune would often turn to the village's shaman, or witch doctor. Africans believed such problems were caused by damage to the person's spiritual relationship with either the supreme god or with a lesser spirit. The witch doctor would attempt to heal the person using natural remedies made from herbs, leaves, roots, fruits, tree barks, insects, eggs, or animal parts.

In some cases, the African might call on a person who is trained to interact with spirits, known as a medium, in order to ask the spirits what he or she did to bring on the sickness. In the African religion, mediums were almost always women. They would allow themselves to be possessed by spirits during a special ritual that involved dancing and drumming. By allowing a spirit to inhabit her body, the medium allowed that spirit to speak directly to the person who was having problems, so the spirit could explain how to appease the spirit world. The medium could also communicate messages and warnings from spirits to the larger community.

In traditional African religions, women known as mediums are specially trained to interact with the spirits. They are believed to be able to help with romantic relationships, remove curses, and ensure success in business or with school exams.

Like all religions, the traditional religions of West Africa offered comfort and hope to those who practiced them. When Africans were uprooted from their homes and sold into slavery, it was a terrible, frightening time. Often, they brought nothing with them to the New World other than their religious beliefs. Despite the efforts of European missionaries to convert the slaves to Christianity, most Africans maintained many of their traditional beliefs.

Typically, African slaves had to practice their religion secretly. In most European colonies of the New World, authorities made those traditional practices illegal, and tried to eliminate them completely. However, one New World city became known for its liberal attitude toward African-American beliefs and practices: New Orleans.

CITY ON THE BAYOU

Since its founding in 1718 by French settlers, New Orleans has always been a place where people with different backgrounds, cultures, and traditions have mingled freely. During the 18th century, New Orleans was home to black slaves who had been brought from many parts of Africa. There were free blacks—some were slaves who had been allowed to purchase their freedom; others had come from the Caribbean islands. There were Native Americans. There were

The oldest part of New Orleans is known as the French Quarter; this neighborhood was the main part of the city when it was founded in 1718. It is known for its architecture, but buildings like this one were actually built between 1764 and 1801, when the city was under the control of the Spanish empire, rather than the French. Many of the original French colonial buildings were destroyed by fires in the city during the 1780s and 1790s.

Slaves brought to the Spanish and French colonies of the New World were often forced to give up their old religion and convert to the Roman Catholic faith. Because certain Catholic practices, such as the veneration of saints, were similar to traditional African religions, slaves in New Orleans were able to blend their animistic practices with those of the officially sanctioned religion.

Europeans from France, Spain, and other countries. And there were mixed-race people who had been born in the New World, and came to be called Creoles.

New Orleans was a French colony from 1718 until 1763, when ownership of the city passed to the Spanish empire. Spain returned the rights to the city to France in 1801, during the Napoleonic wars. In 1803, the government of French emperor Napoleon Bonaparte sold New Orleans, as well the vast Louisiana Territory, to the United States.

During the 18th century, the predominant religion of both France and Spain was Roman Catholicism. That was the major legal religion in New Orleans as well, and slave owners were instructed to convert their slaves to Catholicism. Through religious instruction, the African slaves found some aspects of Catholicism that were similar to their own traditional religions. Africans could equate their creator god with the Christian God. They also accepted the Catholic practice of praying to saints, lighting candles or making offerings to them, and asking them for guidance or to intercede with God. After all, that was basically the same relationship that West Africans had with the spirits of their religion. As a result, in public slaves appeared to have become good, practicing Catholics. In reality, though, they were able to worship their familiar spirits or deities by associating them with a Catholic saint.

New Orleans was unusual because slaves were permitted more freedom there than they received in other colonies in North America. Most slaves did not have to work on Sundays or on religious holidays, and in New Orleans there were public spaces where slaves were allowed to gather on those days. One of those spaces was called the Place des Negres. It would eventually be called Congo Square, and it

The spirits of Voodoo and other religions that originated in West Africa are believed to have distinct personalities. They also have favorite foods, drinks, and colors. Offering alcohol or some other favorite drink to a spirit is a sign of respect and a way to please that spirit.

became a bustling, open-air market, where slaves bought, sold, and traded crafts that they made, or crops that they'd been allowed to grow for themselves. In Congo Square, slaves and free blacks were also allowed to perform traditional African dances, accompanied by drums and stringed instruments.

NEW INFLUENCES

New Orleans was one of several French colonies in North America. France had also established colonies in Canada, as well as on islands like Martinique and Guadeloupe. The French also possessed a colony called Saint-Domingue that covered about one-third of the island of Hispaniola in the Caribbean. By the 1760s, slaves from Africa had turned Saint-Domingue into the most profitable producer of sugar and coffee in the Americas.

As in New Orleans, officials in Saint-Domingue attempted to convert the West African slaves to Roman Catholicism. Just as in New Orleans, the slaves of Saint-Domingue maintained some of their traditional religious practices under the disguise of Catholicism. They also adopted some Native American practices and beliefs. The Africans and their descendants on Saint-Domingue called their religious system Vodou.

Unlike New Orleans, the French government of Saint-Domingue did not tolerate the practice of Vodou. Still, slaves in the colony greatly outnumbered plantation owners and Catholic priests, so the slaves were able to maintain their religious practices in secret. Vodou became a unifying force against the brutal slave system, and Vodou priests played a key role in organizing slaves to revolt during the 1790s. By 1804, the rebels had succeeded in throwing off French rule and gained independence as the country of Haiti.

In Haitian Vodou, spirits are known as *lwas* or *loas*. Each loa is a distinct being with its own personality, and each requires particular songs, dances, and rituals to contact and serve.

Congo Square is listed on the National Register of Historic Places. It is now part of a park that is officially named for jazz musician Louis Armstrong. During the French colonial era, slaves were permitted to gather in the park to sing, dance, perform music, and sell small items.

This illustration from a French book, printed around 1805, shows Haitian soldiers executing French colonial leaders for abuses they committed in the colony. The revolution in Saint-Domingue forced many people to flee the island. A large number made their way to New Orleans, where their Vodou beliefs blended with the existing religious practices of the blacks living there.

Due to the unrest and fighting of this period, thousands of Haitians—including both white plantation owners fleeing the violence and blacks who had escaped slavery—made their way to New Orleans. Haitian Vodou found a home in the city, where it reinforced and blended, or syncretized, with the African-Catholic religions already being practiced there.

Haitian Vodou was not the only belief system that influenced the development of New Orleans Voodoo, however. Visitors to the city from Cuba introduced Santería, a belief system that blended the West African Yorùbá religion with Roman Catholic practices. Another slave religion that influenced the development of Voodoo in New Orleans was Candomblé, which originated in the Portuguese colonies of Brazil. Both Santería and Candomblé were similar to Voodoo because they involved spirit worship, ritual drumming and dancing, and traditional healing. However, they added new elements to New Orleans Voodoo traditions, such as animal sacrifice. Over time New Orleans Voodoo absorbed and incorporated many new elements, the way diverse ethnicities and races were absorbed into the city's population.

HOODOO

In the narrative of his life, the 19th century African-American abolitionist Frederick Douglass told of a time when he was a young slave. He met another slave named Sandy Jenkins, who offered Douglass a way to protect himself from the vicious beatings of a sadistic master by the name of Covey. According to Douglass, "there was a certain root, which, if I would take some of it with me, carrying it always on my right side, would render it impossible for Mr. Covey, or any other white man, to whip me."

Douglass was skeptical, but he tried it anyway. The next day, Covey didn't beat him. The following day, he did. This time, however, Douglass fought back. "[F]rom whence came the spirit I don't know—I resolved to fight," he later wrote. "The whole six months afterwards, that I spent with Mr. Covey, he never laid the weight of his finger upon me in anger."

Frederick Douglass didn't believe that the spirit to fight back came from the "magic" root. He wrote that a belief in root magic was "ignorant, superstitious, and possibly sinful." Many people agreed with him. But many others, both black and white, believed in the power of such magic, which was known as rootwork, conjure, or witchcraft.

Today, the most common name for such magical practices in Louisiana and the southern states is Hoodoo.

Hoodoo is not synonymous with Voodoo, but they are closely related. As a religion, Voodoo involves the worship and honoring of spirits in nature. Hoodoo involves the use of herbs, roots, minerals, and other natural objects to draw on the power of those spirits and create changes in peoples' lives. Practitioners of Voodoo believe that a priest or priestess who is skilled in Hoodoo can create amulets or charms that can help others find love, heal illnesses, provide protection from harm, jinx an enemy, and the like.

ROOTWORK

Herbal healing is not unique to Voodoo. Both Africans and Europeans used bark, leaves, and berries in teas and ointments for hundreds of years. Native Americans who'd been enslaved in Louisiana also had a wide knowledge of plant remedies, which they shared with African slaves.

High John the Conqueror is the root of the white trillium, a white-flowered plant found throughout the eastern United States.

Those who practice New Orleans Voodoo believe that a Voodoo priestess or doctor is inhabited by a spirit while assembling the contents of protective amulets known as gris-gris bags or mojo hands.

Those who practice Voodoo believe that, in addition to their medicinal qualities, some plants possess magical qualities as well. For example, when burned together, absinthe and sandalwood are believed to be useful in conjuring the spirits of the dead. If you want to break up a relationship, sprinkle leaves of the Lemon Verbena shrub at the couple's door, as this will cause them to fight. Patchouli, a type of mint, is an ingredient used in spells to make enemies weak.

No one knows what plant Sandy Jenkins gave to Frederick Douglass to carry for protection, but it might have been a root that is related to the morning glory and the sweet potato. Southerners call this plant High John the Conqueror. It's named for the hero of an African-American folktale, a slave known as John the Conqueror who outwitted his masters and impressed them with his intelligence and

African-American slaves believed that evil spirits were attracted to colored glass bottles, especially blue ones. Once a spirit entered the bottle, it could not get out. Slaves would hang bottles in the trees near their homes as a form of Hoodoo that they believed would protect them from evil spirits. Today, bottle trees can be seen decorating yards and gardens throughout Louisiana and other southern states.

cunning. The High John the Conqueror root is believed to offer powerful magical protection and a way to bring luck and achieve personal mastery over others.

While the entire root can be used for some purposes, vital extracts from plants are often combined into powerful powders. For example, "hot foot powder" was used to get rid of an unwanted person, without doing that person any real harm. The powder is made of hot red pepper, black pepper, and sulfur, mixed with cornstarch or talcum powder. Dirt—sometimes from a graveyard—is often added to disguise its color. Hot foot powder would be sprinkled on the ground where the unwanted person will walk.

Another Hoodoo powder called "goofer dust" was often used to cause trouble and bad luck. In some cases, it was supposed to cause illness or death. Among other things, goofer dust contains graveyard dirt, sulfur, shed snakeskins, powdered bones, and other herbs. Goofer dust would usually be sprinkled around the target's home. When the targeted person stepped in the dust, it would rise up through his or her feet and remain in that person's body. A person who has been "goofered" could lose a job, lose a lover, lose money, or develop a chronic illness. (A person who suspected that he or she had

In Hoodoo, graveyard dirt can be used for both good and bad. It's used in love spells and protection spells, as well as in enemy tricks. When collecting the dirt, the hoodoo worker is said to "buy" it. In the past, the price was a silver dime left at the gravesite.

been goofered could sprinkle salt around the house, as that was supposed to break the jinx.)

CANDLE MAGIC

When practicing Voodoo, candles are often used. They are not just intended to set a mood; instead, candles are believed to be a way to send a message to a spirit or bring about a certain kind of change.

The shapes and sizes of the candles used can vary greatly, from tapers to candles carved in the shape of a figure to small votive candles. One of the most common is the seven-day candle. It's also called a vigil candle, and it burns inside a tall glass "chimney." Due to the

Candles are often used as altar lights, or to complement Hoodoo rituals in which spells are cast.

connection between Voodoo and Roman Catholicism, the chimney often has the image of a saint painted on it.

The colors of candles are also important, as each color has a different meaning:

- White is for protection, healing, and spiritual blessings.
- Blue is for peace, harmony, joy, and health.
- Green candles are used in spells related to money or wealth, such as those meant to bring good luck in gambling, help a person find a job, or ensure a good harvest.
- Red is for love and passion. Red candles are used in love spells and charms.
- Pink is for romance.
- Purple is for power, mastery, and ambition.
- Orange is associated with creativity or a change of plans.
- Brown is for practical matters, such as court cases.
- Yellow is for quick success, mental sharpness, and doing well in school. It's also associated with gold.
- A black candle can be used to send harm or to remove evil. Jinxes, curses, and calling on dark spirits are all associated with black. But black candles can also offer protection from others who might want to cause you harm.

There are also double-action candles that can be turned sideways and burned at both ends. A red and black double-action candle is used to reverse a love jinx; a white and black one is for repelling a curse and returning it to the sender. A green and black double-action candle is for getting rid of a money jinx and bringing money your way. Magical oils, herbs, and flower petals are often used to make candle magic as effective as possible.

Some workers of candle magic say they can read messages in the remains of the candle after it has burned down. Others pay attention to the smoke, and whether the candle or its glass chimney gets sooty or stays clean. Still others believe it's the flame that provides the message.

MAGIC BUNDLES

In 1806, a French visitor to West Africa wrote, "[The natives of Senegal] place implicit faith in the efficacy of a talisman, which they call gris-gris: they wear it round their neck, at their waist, and on their legs and arms." Those West Africans who were shipped to Louisiana

HOODOO RECIPES

Those who practice New Orleans Voodoo and Hoodoo have many different "recipes." Here are a few sample Hoodoo measures that are intended to bring a person love, luck, money, or afflict their enemies.

To Harm an Enemy (Marie Laveau): Place the name of your enemy on a slip of paper and place it in the mouth of a snake. Hang the snake out in the sun to dry. As the snake suffers, so does your enemy.

To Protect Yourself From Spells: Walk around the house with a lighted blessed candle or throw salt into the corners of each room of your house. The process will uncross most spells.

For Love: Burn a blue candle lighted by 7 matches. To get love from the person you desire, light the candle daily and sprinkle Van Van oil for 9 days on the lighted blue candle.

To Protect Your Health: Tie a cord that has 3, 7, or 9 knots around your waist for overall protection.

To Keep a Lover Faithful: Write the person's name on a piece of paper and put it up the chimney. Pray to it three times a day.

To Shorten an Enemy's Life: Wave a broom over a person's body to shorten their lifespan.

Voodoo dolls are perhaps the best known form of gris-gris. Often, the dolls include something from the person that the doll is supposed to represent, such as a lock of hair or a personal item. This is believed to give the voodoo doll more power.

as slaves continued to believe in the power of talismans, despite their harsh life on the plantations.

Gris-gris bags are also called by different names, such as mojo hands or conjure sacks. Whatever the name, they're considered to be among the most powerful charms in the world of Voodoo. In the early days, they were made from a leather bag. If the person was from a country with a Muslim influence, the bag might contain a verse from the Qur'an. If the person observed a Christian religion, a small cross or a holy medal might be placed inside. Bits of human bone, dust from a grave, bird feathers, herbs, roots, and even goofer dust might be placed inside. These were believed to confer various powers, such as protection from evil, financial success, good luck, or love.

During the 18th and 19th centuries, gris-gris bags became common in and around New Orleans. Slaves would hide them underneath their clothing, so they would not be denounced for practicing African witchcraft. This probably resulted in the Voodoo belief that letting someone else touch or see a gris-gris bag would make it lose its power.

Gris-gris bags are still small today, and they're almost always made of flannel. Red is the color of choice, but almost any color will do.

To function properly, a gris-gris bag has to be kept strong. In Hoodoo, this is known as "feeding the mojo hand." One of the most common ways of doing this is to anoint the sack with a few drops of magic oil from time to time. The type of oil would depend on the purpose of the bag. Rum, whiskey, or certain perfumes could be used as well.

VOODOO DOLLS

The Voodoo doll is a well-known form of gris-gris, in which a Voodoo doctor or priestess fashions a doll intended to represent a particular person. These dolls can be used to invoke the spirits and ask them to affect the person that the doll represents. Practitioners of Voodoo believe these dolls can be used for love, for power and domination, for luck, for uncrossing spells and jinxes and, yes, in some evil ways, for doing harm.

The idea of Voodoo dolls probably originated from wooden, human-shaped figurines called Minkisi that the people of West and Central Africa traditionally created. These figurines were thought to capture the spirit of the dead, so that living people could use them to counteract evil spirits and malign powers in the world. Often, these figurines have nails or pieces of metal driven into them. These are meant to give the spirit a way to travel between its world and the human world. Pouches filled with different magical herbs were attached to or inserted into the figurine.

Traditionally, Voodoo dolls were made by tying colored cloth

Voodoo dolls also share a history with poppets, small dolls usually sewn from cloth. Poppets originated in Europe and were used in European witchcraft; they were well known to the French settlers of New Orleans.

Gris-gris sounds like a French phrase, but it probably isn't. In French, the word *gris* means "gray." It is more likely that the term for this amulet may have come from the Mande tribe of West Africa, which called them *gerregerys*. Similarly, the word *mojo* was probably derived from *moco'o*, a word in the Fulani language that means "medicine man."

around a wooden spoon. The cloth would be stuffed with Spanish moss, as well as magical herbs. The face was generally left blank. This way, the person using it could draw in the features, or pin a picture of the person the doll is intended to represent. A lock of hair or fingernail clippings from the person might be enclosed in the doll, to give it greater power.

Scary Hollywood movies involving Voodoo often include these magical dolls, sometimes with an evil Voodoo doctor sticking pins or nails into it to cause an actual person to feel pain. Practitioners of Voodoo point out that poking a doll with a pin does not really cause the person pain at the same moment. Instead, the doll is simply used to appeal to the spirits on the user's behalf.

Voodoo Heyday

New Orleans was booming in the early 19th century. Cotton, rice, and sugar were in high demand throughout the United States, and much of it was shipped through the growing port city near the mouth of the Mississippi River. The city was a bustling, busy place with a fascinating mix of cultures and heritages. It featured a wide range of entertainment, from theater and opera to gambling dens, bars, and music halls.

By this time Voodoo had gone from being an obscure religious practice to a visible part of the New Orleans "scene." White residents and curious out-of-towners alike went to see the dancing and drumming at Congo Square. Often, a variety of amulets, love charms, powders and potions were for sale in the square.

In private, people continued to seek the help and advice of those who practiced Voodoo. In New Orleans, male spiritual leaders were usually referred to as "doctor," while women called themselves "priestess" or "queen." These spiritual leaders were paid to conduct

A plaque, pennies, and scratched X's adorn the reputed tomb of voodoo queen Marie Laveau in the St. Louis Cemetery in New Orleans. Throughout the years people have come to this tomb to scratch an 'X' and leave an offering to pay their respects to the voodoo queen.

ritual ceremonies and petition the spirits on behalf of their clients. They also provided medicinal remedies, cast spells intended to bring luck, and foretold the future.

In general, the Voodoo queens or priestesses had the greatest influence. Some of the more prominent early 19th century Voodoo queens included Sainte DeDe, Marie Saloppe, and Marie Comptesse. Not much is known about them today. Sainte DeDe was a freewoman of color from Santo Domingo. She probably sold food and performed Voodoo rituals in her courtyard. According to the stories, her home was near a cathedral, and people attending mass could hear the beating of the drums.

But there is one 19th century Voodoo queen who hasn't been forgotten.

Marie Laveau

Although Marie Laveau has been dead for more than 130 years, she remains a New Orleans legend. In fact, her tomb in the city's historic burial ground, St. Louis Cemetery No. 1, is one of the most-visited graves in the United States. Every day, people visit the crypt to ask Laveau—New Orleans's most prominent Voodoo queen from the 1820s to the 1870s—to grant their wishes.

Marie Laveau was born in the French Quarter of New Orleans, probably in 1801. Her parents are believed to have been mixed-race

Drawing of a New Orleans Voodoo ceremony that appeared in an 1887 issue of Harper's Magazine.

(probably African and French), but not slaves. No photographs or pictures exist to show what Marie looked like as a young woman, but she was supposedly tall and very beautiful. She apparently earned a living as a hairdresser for several years, and was a devout Roman Catholic.

In 1819, Laveau married a free Haitian named Jacques Paris, but the marriage did not last long. No one is sure whether he died or simply abandoned her and returned to Haiti. By 1826 Marie was in a relationship with a wealthy white man named Louis Christophe Glapion. They had at least seven children together.

Laveau's work probably helped build her reputation as a Voodoo queen. As a hairdresser, Laveau would have heard a lot of gossip

This portrait of Marie Laveau was painted in the 1920s. It is based on a painting made by the American artist George Catlin during the 1830s, which has since been lost. The portrait above is part of the Louisiana State Museum collection.

and secrets from her clients. Some of them were wealthy white or creole women; others were their servants or slaves. When they told Marie their problems, she probably proposed Voodoo charms or remedies to solve them. Soon she had a network of clients, from all social levels, who trusted in her ability to intervene with the spirits and guide their lives.

Laveau probably also used the information she heard from her clients to make accurate predictions when asked by others to tell the future. Apparently, she sometimes employed blackmail and intimidation to make her predictions come true. According to one tale, when a man asked Marie to predict his future, she foretold that he would soon get a particular job. Then, she visited a local politician and threatened to publicly reveal what she had heard about his secret activities unless he offered her client the position. The job-seeker paid Laveau for the spookily successful prediction and told others about it, enhancing her reputation. A side benefit was that she also now had ties to a politician who was afraid to cross her.

Word spread about her "magical" healing potions and her accurate predictions. By the late 1820s, Marie Laveau was a major presence at Congo Square every Sunday, selling love charms and potions and offering private services and consultations to crowds who came to watch. Although not the only Voodoo queen at the time, she was easily the most successful, and crowds of her admirers often drove competing spiritual leaders away. Some stories say that Laveau was the

St. John's Eve, June 23, is observed the night before the Roman Catholic Feast of St. John the Baptist on June 24. Those days are significant because they coincide with the summer solstice, the longest day of the year. The tradition of holding bonfires on St. John's Eve goes back to pagan times, and was originally meant to ensure a good harvest.

first Voodoo queen to entertain crowds with a large snake, which she called Zombi.

It had long been rumored in New Orleans that Voodoo practitioners held secret ceremonies on the shores of nearby Lake Pontchartrain or in Bayou St. John. In the 1830s, Marie Laveau began inviting the public to attend the Voodoo ceremony at the lake on St. John's Eve, June 23. She charged admission to the thousands of curious people who attended. For those who believed in Voodoo, St. John's Eve was a religious, spiritual occasion. For the curious onlookers, it was a show and Marie Laveau was its star. And for Marie Laveau, it was an opportunity to make a nice profit.

Whether she was a true spiritual leader, a con artist, or a little of both, there is no doubt that Marie Laveau increased the visibility of New Orleans Voodoo. However, she was also greatly respected in New Orleans. There are many stories of Marie taking care of the sick when the city experienced epidemics of yellow fever and cholera, or offering care and spiritual comfort to prisoners on death row.

Laveau started to retire from public life in 1869, although she continued to meet with clients until the mid-1870s. By the time Marie died in 1881, she had become so famous that newspapers across the country, including the *New York Times*, published her obituary. The Times called her "one of the most wonderful women who ever lived," while another newspaper made a prediction: "Marie Laveau's name will not be forgotten in New Orleans."

That prediction turned out to be true.

OTHER NOTABLE VOODOO PERSONALITIES

While Marie Laveau remains one of the best-known people of Voodoo, she is far from the only one. In fact, one of her daughters followed in her footsteps in the late 19th century. Known as Marie Laveau II (1827–1895), she managed some of her mother's properties, including a mansion known as Maison Blanche where secret Voodoo meetings were held, along with lavish parties. The police never raided these parties, allegedly because they were afraid Marie would put a curse on them.

KNOCK THREE TIMES

Recently, a woman who had been diagnosed with a serious illness traveled from New York to New Orleans to make an offering at the tomb of Marie Laveau. After what she called a nearly complete recovery, she visited the tomb again. "If you believe there are spiritual forces with great power," she explained, "this is definitely a place to come."

Whether they believe in a powerful spiritual force or are just curious, people continue to flock to Marie Laveau's tomb, the way both the curious and spiritual flocked to her ceremonies on Bayou St. John when she was alive.

The tomb is located in St. Louis Cemetery No. 1, the oldest cemetery in the city. Residents of New Orleans often call the cemeteries "cities of the dead." Tombs are built above ground because early settlers discovered very quickly that after a hard rain, coffins buried in the swampy ground would float to the surface.

The tomb where Marie Laveau is believed to be buried is hard to miss. X's have been drawn all over it—some in red brick dust, some in chalk or charcoal, some even in lipstick. Cemetery caretakers and tour guides discourage the practice because people sometimes remove bricks from nearby graves to draw the marks, and lipstick isn't easily removed. The gravesite is cleaned regularly and funds are raised to help keep it up.

But the tradition continues: draw an X, knock three times on the slab at the foot of the tomb, turn three times, and make a petition to Marie Laveau's spirit. Leave a small offering of coins, flowers, candy, candles, even an alcoholic beverage. If your wish is granted, return to the grave and draw a circle around the X mark that you left.

A man named Jean Montenet became one of the most feared Voodoo doctors in New Orleans. He was born around 1815; according to stories he told, he had been a member of a royal family in Senegal, but was captured by slave traders as a young man. After being sold to a sugar plantation in Cuba, he somehow managed to talk his owner into setting him free, then he sailed the world as a ship's cook. When he finally stopped sailing, he worked on the docks in New Orleans and made the city his home.

While working on the docks, Jean gained a reputation for being able to predict the future. He could do this, it was said, by reading marks on the bales of cotton being loaded onto ships. No one knows exactly how he did it, but many of his predictions came true. As his reputation spread, both blacks and whites began coming to him for predictions and advice. He became known around New Orleans as Doctor John or Voodoo John (Jean is the French version of "John").

Telling the future paid well enough for Doctor John to buy a large piece of land and build a house. Eventually, Doctor John began to offer his clients potions as well as predictions. His reputation grew, and so did his income. He became one of the wealthiest blacks in New Orleans. He was also known for helping care for the sick during epidemics, and for helping members of the African-American community in need.

Today, some people believe Doctor John was a fraud. They think that like Marie Laveau, he developed a network of slaves in wealthy households who acted as spies for him, telling him secrets that he could use for fortune telling, or maybe even as blackmail. As evidence that he did not really have magical powers, they point out that he eventually lost all his property and died a poor man in 1885. If he

Mac "Dr. John" Rebenack, a New Orleans musician, took his name from the Dr. John of Voodoo fame, after discovering that one of his distant ancestors had been related to the original Dr. John. Rebenack's first album was titled *Gris Gris*.

A drum that was often played at Congo square was the bamboula, a long narrow African drum that probably originated in West Africa. It's made of bamboo with skin stretched over it and comes in different lengths. The word "bamboula" is also used to describe a rhythm and a dance.

could truly predict the future, why did he not just select the winning numbers in the Havana lottery to replenish his fortune, they say? No one knows for sure. But enough people had faith in his abilities that Doctor John remains probably the best-known Voodoo doctor of the time.

In the 1860s, a slave who called himself Dr. Yah Yah gained a reputation in New Orleans for his potions. They were reputed to cure

Photo taken in the early 1930s of a Voodoo practitioner named Louie dancing during a ceremony. Louie's wife Lala was a well-known New Orleans Voodoo queen in the early 20th century.

physical ailments such as rheumatism. Supposedly, his favorite cure-all blended jimpson weed, honey, sulphur, and other ingredients. To be effective, this elixir had to be drunk from a glass that had been rubbed against a black cat.

Healing potions combined with the magic of Voodoo was exotic and mysterious, and brought Dr. Yah Yah a lot of clients. However, when he tried to give the remedy to one white plantation owner, the man's doctor checked out the potion and recognized the jimpson weed, which can be toxic to humans. The slave was accused of trying to poison the slaveowner, and was punished severely.

NEW ORLEANS VOODOO TODAY

In 1886, a reporter wrote, "As a religion—an imported faith—Voudooism in Louisiana is really dead; the rites of its serpent worship are forgotten; the meaning of its strange and frenzied chants, whereof some fragments linger as refrains in negro song, is not now known even to those who remember the words; and the story of its former existence is only revealed to the folklorists by the multitudinous debris of African superstition which it has left behind it."

The "debris of African superstitions" that the writer denounced—dolls and other fetishes, gris-gris bags, and magic oils—could still be found in the city. Voodoo was one of the things that attracted visitors to New Orleans. The dancing and drumming at Congo Square began to develop sounds that would influence jazz and other forms of music during the 20th century.

But the point of his article was to question whether people still truly believed in New Orleans Voodoo as a religion. By the late 19th century, many people dismissed Voodoo as a tourist-driven business. Shops and stores sold gris-gris bags and Voodoo dolls, and self-styled

Visitors to New Orleans can find Voodoo-related items, such as charms and gris-gris bags, sold as souvenirs in many stores. However, there are people in New Orleans who continue to practice Voodoo as a serious religion.

doctors and queens made money casting spells or hexing people.

Many people believe the same thing is true now. Many of the people who today conduct Voodoo services for believers also own shops that sell Voodoo-related items such as candles and herbs. They say they have to make a living, but the business side of Voodoo doesn't mean that they aren't genuinely faithful.

New Orleans Voodoo as a religion isn't dead or forgotten. It's just different.

WHAT IS THE REAL VOODOO?

The members of the temple eased the priestess to the floor as she trembled from the possession. A few moments passed in tense silence and then the priestess raised her head. The shaking was gone, replaced by calm determination. Her eyes intensely explored the temple and the faces of the faithful. Dutifully, they brought her the offerings of corn, rum and meat. For the priestess was no longer herself. The fiery spirit Ezili Dantor, a Haitian Vodou lwa, had possessed her.

This ritual of possession took place in New Orleans, not during the 19th century but in the 21st. It was a Haitian ceremony. Haitian Vodou has become integrated with New Orleans Voodoo more strongly than ever. Rather than dying out, Voodoo has simply adapted and changed.

Today, many of those who practice New Orleans Voodoo are white. And not all of them are natives of New Orleans, either. Sallie Ann Glassman, for example, was born in Maine and brought up in the

It's not possible to draw a straight line between the West African music once heard in Congo Square and today's jazz. But many original New Orleans jazz musicians had a connection to Congo Square or to Voodoo. The famed trumpeter and jazz performer Louis Armstrong remembered his grandmother telling him about how she danced in Congo Square in the 19th century. Today, Congo Square lies within an open area of the city known as Louis Armstrong Park, which was created to honor the city's rich jazz music history.

Bayou St. John, where Marie Laveau and others held Voodoo ceremonies during the 19th century, looks much different now. Much of the bayou was drained and filled in during the 1930s. However, ceremonies are still held on the Magnolia Bridge, a pedestrian walkway that crosses the bayou. Here, Voodoo Priestess Sallie Ann Glassman conducts a St. John's Eve ritual.

Jewish faith. After studying Vodou in New Orleans and then in Haiti, she was initiated into the religion and became a manbo, or priestess. Today, she practices her faith in New Orleans, conducting ceremonies and rituals for the faithful. But many of her ceremonies are open and advertised to the public, including one on St. John's Eve. To her, Voodoo is a healing, open religion, and she welcomes all who are interested.

Others have taken a more individualized approach to the practices that Voodoo encompasses. For example, Brenda Marie Osbey, Louisiana's Poet Laureate from 2005 to 2007 and a professor at Brown University, practices her faith in private. She doesn't call it Voodoo; to

View of a Voodoo altar, with offerings of money and alcohol for the spirits.

This representation of a Voodoo doll ornaments a balcony in the French Quarter during the annual Mardi Gras celebration in New Orleans.

Interest in Voodoo was revived in 1932, when the movie *White Zombie* came out. Zombies had nothing to do with New Orleans Voodoo; the idea of the zombie as an animated undead creature originated in Haiti. And Haitians weren't afraid of zombies; they were afraid of becoming zombies, because that would mean they had no soul or will. But that didn't matter. Movie zombies were scary, and many people who saw the movie came to believe they were an integral part of New Orleans Voodoo.

her and to other believers from New Orleans, it's simply known as "The Religion." People must be born into The Religion and raised in it. Its focus, she says, is restoring balance and honoring ancestors and loved ones. Connection to the spirit world is made through altars and prayers to the saints, who relay messages to the dead. And it's done in private, with home altars. There is no need for public gatherings or rituals.

FINDING VOODOO

The author of a recently published guidebook to New Orleans writes, "Voodoo is still widely practiced today. Like New Orleans's high water table, it lies just below the topsoil of daily life." According to the statistics compiled by the New Orleans Historical Voodoo Museum, today about 15 percent of the population of New Orleans practices Voodoo in one form or another.

There is no doubt that Voodoo remains a major draw for tourists. Visitors to New Orleans will find many shops selling Voodoo dolls and gris-gris bags, or ingredients for magical Voodoo potions and instructions on how to use them. Each day, tours take hundreds of visitors to Marie Laveau's tomb, Congo Square, and other Voodoo-related sites. But even in these places, a visitor can find hints of the "real" Voodoo. For example, many of the shops have altars, where tourists can leave coins or light candles. To most people, using those altars is simply a fun thing to do, sort of like tossing a penny into a wishing well. But true believers do use those altars, leaving offerings for a particular spirit or saint.

Jerry Gandolfo, owner of the New Orleans Historical Voodoo Museum, says that practitioners of Voodoo often use the altar in the museum's Occult Room. They leave offerings such as candles, packs of sugar, small bottles of rum, or written messages.

Brenda Marie Osbey has said that because of the unfair stigma attached to Voodoo, "Some people raised in The Religion may no longer feel comfortable having an altar in their own home, but instead use the altar at the museum to honor their ancestors."

True to its beginnings in New Orleans, Voodoo has adapted and changed. But whether on the surface or below the topsoil, it remains alive and well in New Orleans.

APPENDIX
A VOODOO OPENING CEREMONY

Editor's note: during the Great Depression in the 1930s, a federal government agency called the Works Progress Administration (WPA) was created to provide jobs for millions of Americans. One of the WPA projects involved interviewing older Americans, particularly former slaves, and preserving their stories and folklore. This description of the ceremony to initiate someone into the Voodoo culture of New Orleans was produced by the Louisiana Works Progress Administration, and is part of the WPA collection at the State Library of Louisiana. It is called an opening ceremony because it "opens" a person and makes them able to communicate with the spirits.

The opening was done in a very dark room in the rear of the house. We had a small fire that soon went out, after which the room was very dark and unpleasant. However, we were not permitted to complain about it. There were only four of us at the opening, "Grandma," Nom, Miss Breaux, and the writer.

First, Nom made an altar on the floor with a white cloth (it was clean and pressed, about the size of an average table cloth). He placed St. Peter's picture on the cloth. This picture was used because St. Peter opens the gates of heaven. Green and white candles were lit on the cloth, rather, slightly off the cloth; other candles were placed around the picture. Nom placed two quart-sized bottles on the altar, one of cider and the other of raspberry pop. Several plates were put on the altar. In one plate was some steel dust which was on the right side of the picture, oris root powder was placed in front of the picture, a plate of dry basile was in the center of the picture and to the front near the center was a plate of stage planks (cake) and a box of ginger snaps. To the left of the cakes was a plate of mixed bird seed. To the rear of this was a plate of cloves; to the right was cinnamon. On each side of this were the pans of con-gris, which was cooked red beans and rice. A small bottle of olive oil was to the left of the picture with a bag of sugar to the left of this, slightly off of the cloth or altar. There was a bunch of bananas on the left side and some apples on the right. After arranging the powders, etc., Nom placed a piece of camphor branch near the picture, also a glass of bastile. The camphor represented a palm. A half pint of gin was placed in the center front while a bottle of Jax beer was put to the left of the picture.

Just after the altar was arranged, Nom started undressing in a manner very startling. First he took off his coat, then vest, shirt, and finally, his shoes. He rolled up his trousers. Two chairs were placed facing the altar. Miss Breaux sat in one and the writer in the other. "Grandma" was just a few feet away in another chair. Nom stood up and commanded that the writer take off his coat while both the writer and Miss Breaux had to take off their shoes and socks and stockings. The three pairs of shoes were placed on the altar along with a court eviction notice that belonged to Nom. A small wash tub was placed in front of the altar. In it Nom put gin, cider, raspberry, steel dust, in fact everything that was on the altar, save the cake and fruit. He stirred the mixture up well with his hand.

We knelt on one knee on the floor. Nom had his head in his hand and prayed in French. We knocked on the floor with our right hand loud but very slowly. This was done to call the spirits. All of us said the Lord's Prayer slowly. Nom worked himself into a frenzy by singing and praying in French. He made all kinds of peculiar motions at the same time. He drank a large drink and went into a semi-trance. Nom grunted, hollered, and called on the spirits for assistance. After every drink of gin Nom would act like a man going crazy with all kinds of dances and prayers. It really got good to him, so good that he did not seem to know just where he was. Nom often spit some of the gin in his hand and rubbed it on his head and face.

Nom next put Miss Breaux on his back and turned her around three times. First, she was turned under his arms and then swayed on his back. The writer went through the same procedure but with more action. The writer was hit on his pants pocket three times and had to keep his hands there for about ten minutes. He spit the gin in his hands and later shook ours. Miss Breaux was again turned around. During the time of the turning we were to ask for the power to do the kind of work desired. Our feet and legs were washed with the mixture in the tub. Nom passed the lighted candles over his face and through his mouth several times. The candles were put out with his mouth. Miss Breaux was given a white lighted candle for good luck and green candle for money. Miss Breaux's candles were notched three times. She was instructed to burn the candle at three different occasions, each time asking for what may be desired. The writer was given a red candle, broken in three parts. He was told to burn it and ask for anything that is wanted. The red candle was one for evil. It had been passed through Nom's mouth several times. He bit off the bottom of the green candle and instructed that the writer light it at the bitten end, stating that this would make all of my enemies upset. Nom rubbed steel dust, dry basile, and cinnamon on the inside of our shoes. The shoes were also rubbed with the mixture that was in the tub. He spitted in the shoes of the writer and washed Miss Breaux's stockings with gin. Nom next offered us a sip of gin but we refused. The bottle was put to our mouths, after which, he washed Miss Breaux's hair with gin.

Nom gave some of the material that was on the altar. Miss Breaux was given apples to throw away to something smaller than she. She was instructed to throw it and some cake over her shoulder, making a wish while doing this. Birds were said to want the cakes. Nom explained that the bird represents the dove, which represents Our Lord. Miss Breaux was given some of the mixture in the tub; told to strain it and sell some for luck water. Nom said that she could get $5 per bottle for it. "It would be good to wash your steps," he said. The writer was given dry basile to keep in his pocket for good luck. We were told to give the bananas to little children, preferably poor.

Nom explained that everything must be done in threes to represent the Father, Son, and Holy Ghost.

Nom was paid $2 for the opening, which is absolutely necessary for anyone to be a hoodoo queen or doctor. Nom said that we were free to practice hoodoo and that he would be very pleased to help us at any time free of charge.

We went to the graveyards later, and did practically the same thing as we did the previous time. Incidentally, the opening was done as 12:00 noon on Wednesday. Nom contended that Wednesdays are the best time for openings.

CHRONOLOGY

1718: French settlers establish the city of New Orleans in the Louisiana territory.

1719: Shiploads of slaves begin to arrive in New Orleans. Most of the slaves were originally from West Africa, and brought their religious beliefs with them.

1763: At the end of the Seven Year's War, France cedes control of New Orleans to Spain.

1789: St. Louis Cemetery No. 1 is opened in New Orleans. Today, it is the oldest and most famous burial ground still in existence.

1801: France regains control over the city of New Orleans.

1803: The United States purchases the Louisiana Territory from France, and New Orleans falls under American control.

1804: Slave revolutions in the French colony of Saint-Domingue succeed in overthrowing French government, and the country of Haiti is established. Tens of thousands of people fleeing the unrest in Haiti move to New Orleans, where their religious beliefs (Vodou) blend with New Orleans Voodoo.

1822: The Girod Street Cemetery in New Orleans is opened.

1830: Marie Laveau becomes the dominant figure of Voodoo, publicizing and profiting from the religion through festivals and ceremonies. She would maintain a high profile until the late 1860s.

1881: Marie Laveau dies, and is buried in the Glapion family crypt in St. Louis Cemetery No. 1.

1932: The film *White Zombie* opens in movie theaters, drawing attention to Voodoo.

1971: A portion of the old Girod Street Cemetery is unearthed during construction of the New Orleans Superdome.

1978: Fred Staten, a modern-day Voodoo doctor known as Prince Keeyama or Chicken Man, dies in New Orleans.

1983: Bianca, a descendant of Marie Laveau, is given the title of Voodoo Queen in New Orleans.

2000: Ava Kay Jones, a New Orleans Voodoo priestess, conducts a Voodoo ceremony at the Superdome before an NFL playoff game to appease the spirits and lift their "curse." Her attempt is apparently successful, as the New Orleans Saints win the game and go on to future playoff successes.

GLOSSARY

amulet—an object, such as a medallion or gris-gris bag, that is believed to have the power to protect its possessor from harm.

bamboula—a kind of drum made from a large hollow piece of bamboo with skin stretched over the ends. The word *bamboula* can also be used to describe a dance performed by Africans to the sound of the drums.

elixir—a potion that is intended to be drunk, so that it can have a curative effect on the user.

goofer dust—a powder that is used by some practitioners of Voodoo to cast spells and curse enemies. It is part of the hoodoo tradition in New Orleans.

gris-gris—a charm or amulet of African origin used by practitioners of Voodoo to protect them from harm. These are often small bags that contain a variety of materials. Gris-gris are sometimes referred to as "mojo hands."

Hoodoo—a name for African-American folk magic, often performed with roots, plants, candles, amulets, dust, and other substances.

Jimpson weed—a strong-smelling, poisonous weed of the nightshade family with large, trumpet-shaped white flowers.

lwas—in Haitian Vodou, spirits who are involved with human concerns. These spirits are also known as *loas*.

minkisi—in African traditional religions, these are objects that a spirit inhabits.

rheumatism—a disease causing inflammation of the joints and muscles.

stigma—something with a negative association attached to it.

syncretized—when several beliefs from several different religious systems are blended or harmonized to create a new religious system.

Vodou—the name for an African religion that emerged on the island of Haiti in the 17th and 18th centuries. It is similar to New Orleans Voodoo in some respects, and influenced the development of Voodoo.

FURTHER READING

Alvarado, Denise. *The Voodoo Hoodoo Spellbook*. San Francisco: Red Wheel/Weiser LLC, 2011.

Bodin, Ron. *Voodoo: Past and Present.* Lafayette: Center for Louisiana Studies, 1990.

Filan, Kenaz. *The New Orleans Voodoo Handbook*. Rochester: Destiny Books, 2011.

Long, Carolyn Morrow. *Spiritual Merchants: Religion, Magic, and Commerce*. Knoxville: University of Tennessee Press, 2001.

———. *A New Orleans Voudou Priestess: The Legend and Reality of Marie Laveau*. Gainesville: University Press of Florida, 2007.

Ward, Martha. *Voodoo Queen: The Spirited Lives of Marie Laveau*. Jackson: University Press of Mississippi, 2004.

INTERNET RESOURCES

www.nps.gov/ethnography/aah/aaheritage/histcontextsa.htm

At this page, the National Park Service provides information about West Africa. The superstitions and religious beliefs of slaves from this region formed the basis for Voodoo beliefs.

www.voodoomuseum.com

The website of the New Orleans Historic Voodoo Museum contains articles and information about Voodoo practices and important personalities.

www.luckymojo.com/hoodoohistory.html

The essay "Hoodoo, Conjure, and Rootwork" by Catherine Yronwode provides insights into the history of Hoodoo.

www.voodoospiritualtemple.org/home.html

The Voodoo Spiritual Temple, led by Priestess Miriam Chamani, focuses on spiritual and herbal healing practices.

www.haitianconsulate.org/vodou.html

Interesting information on the history and practice of Haitian Vodou is available at the website of the Consulate General of Haiti in the United States.

INDEX

Numbers in **bold italic** refer to captions.

ABOUT
THE AUTHOR

Carol Ellis has written many books for young people, both fiction and non-fiction, as well as classroom educational materials such as reading comprehension workbooks. In history, she has written about Ancient Greece, the Gilded Age, African American activists and artists, the history and development of Hip Hop and Rap, and the development of the military in Colonial America.

PHOTO CREDITS: Library of Congress: 12, 22, 38, 45; Louisiana State Museum, New Orleans: 7 (inset), 39; used under license from Shutterstock, Inc.: 3, 8, 18, 24, 26, 27, 28, 29, 30, 32, 33, 37; Aneese / Shutterstock.com: 7 (main); Ariadna22822 / Shutterstock.com: 16; Jorg Hackemann / Shutterstock.com: 17, 46; Anton Ivanov / Shutterstock.com: 44; Wendy Kaveney Photography / Shutterstock.com: 50 (bottom); Lemon Tree Images / Shutterstock.com: 40; Dietmar Temps / Shutterstock.com: 14; Urosr / Shutterstock.com: 15; NewOrleansOnline.com: 10; David Richmond/NewOrleansOnline.com: 21; Michael Terranova/NewOrleansOnline.com: 9; Bart Everson/Wikimedia Commons: 49; Greg Wills: 50 (top).